I See Patterns

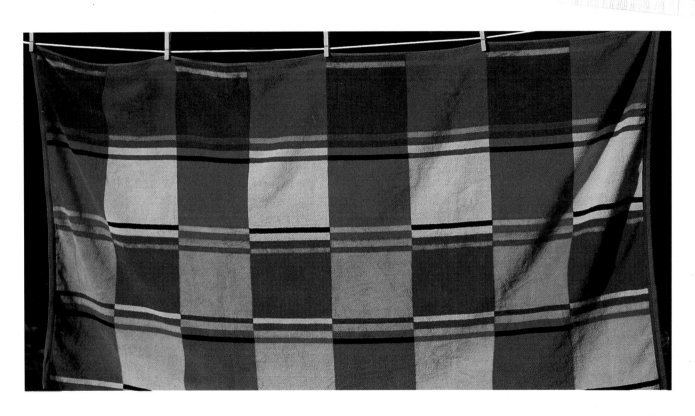

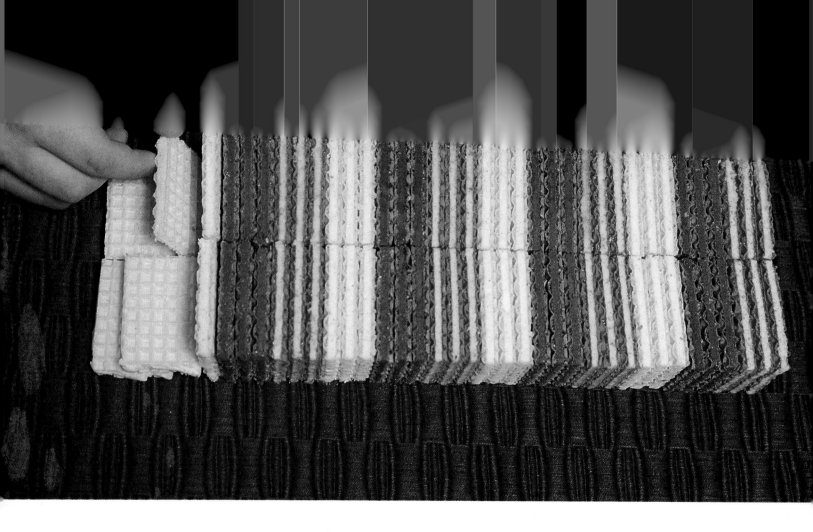

I see patterns on the cookies.

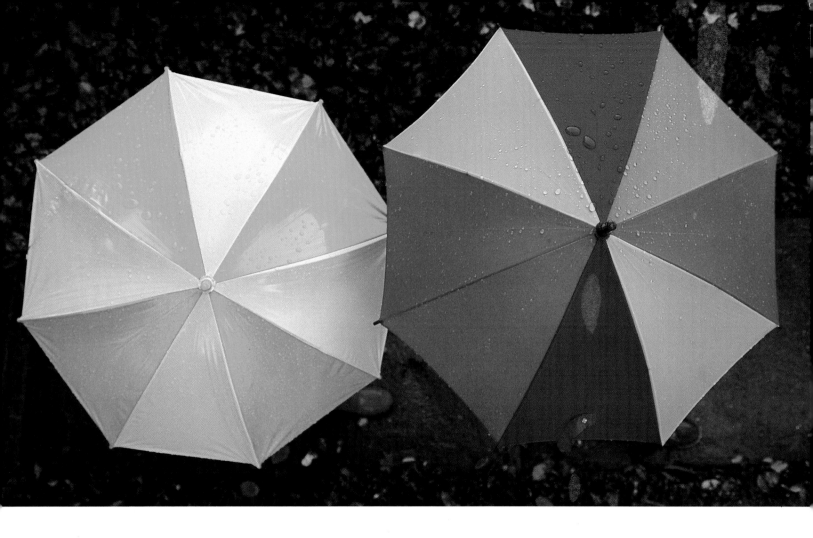

I see patterns on the umbrellas.

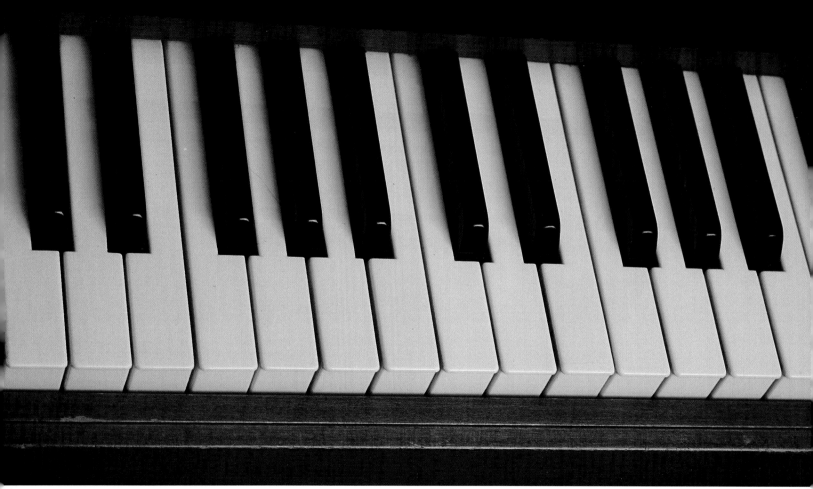

4 I see patterns on the piano.

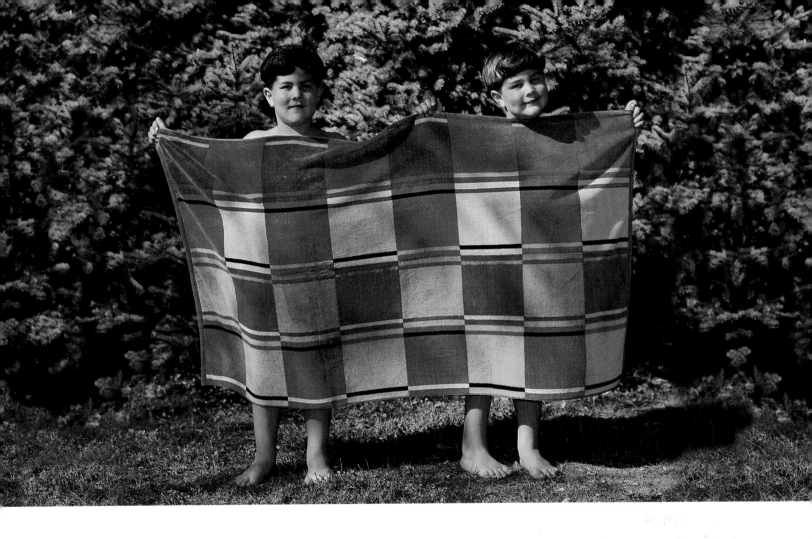

I see patterns on the beach towel.

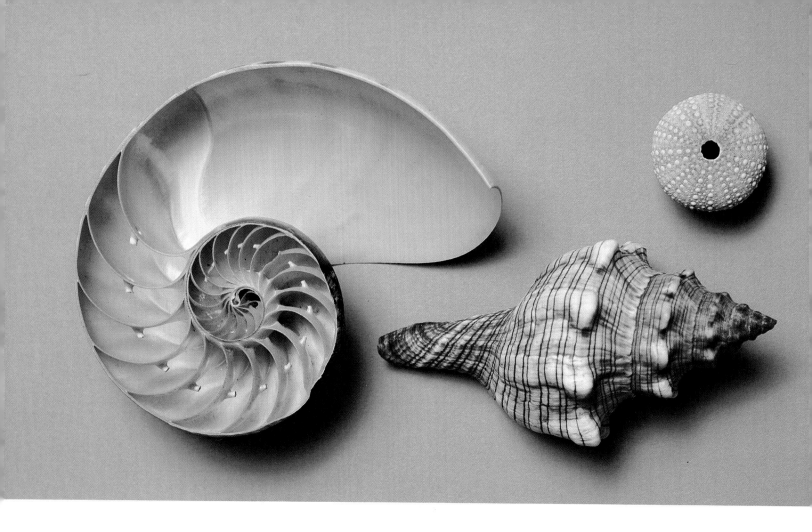

I see patterns on the shells.

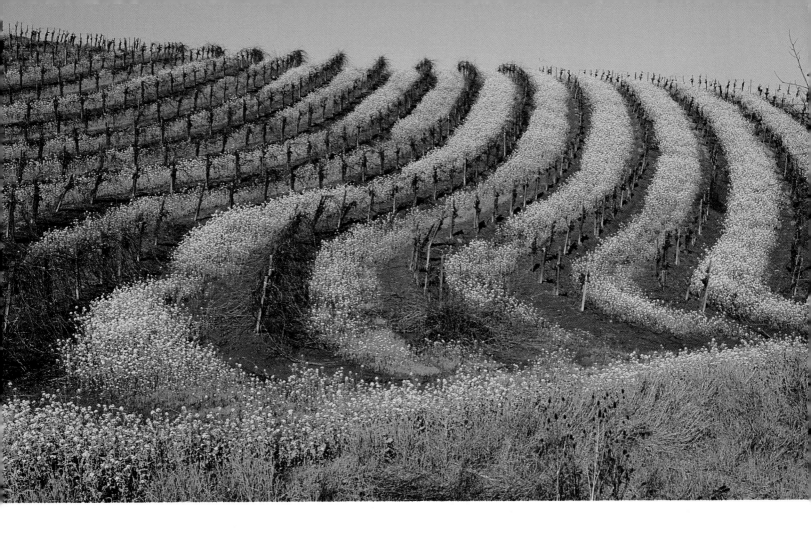

I see patterns on the hill.

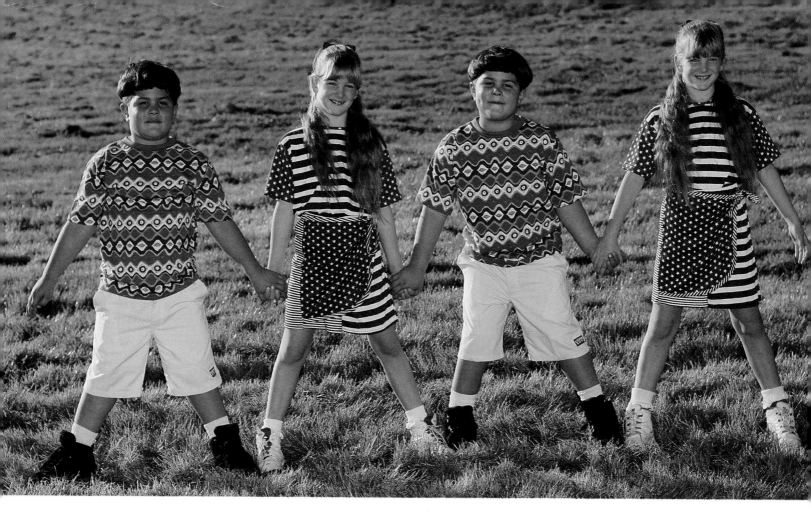

I see patterns on me!